THE CHRISTMAS STORY FOR CHILDREN

Written by
MAX LUCADO, RANDY FRAZEE, AND KAREN DAVIS HILL

Illustrated by
FAUSTO BIANCHI

ZONDERKIDZ

The Christmas Story for Children
Copyright © 2014 by Max Lucado, Randy Frazee, and Karen Davis Hill
Illustrations © 2014 by Fausto Bianchi

Requests for information should be addressed to:

ZonderKidz, 3900 *Sparks Drive SE, Grand Rapids, Michigan* 49546

ISBN 978-0-310-73598-4

Editor: Mary Hassinger
Art direction: Kris Nelson
Design: Cindy Davis
Illustrator: Fausto Bianchi, represented by Beehive Illustration
Artwork colorist: Steve James

Printed in China

14 15 16 17 /DSC/ 16 15 14 13 12 11 10 9 8 7 6 5 4 3 2 1

For our grandchildren—

*"You will become pregnant and give
birth to a son. You must name him Jesus."*

Luke 1:31 NCV

—The Authors

The Jewish people, God's special people, settled in their land. Hundreds of years passed. Generations were born, grew up, and died, and great kingdoms rose and fell.

And the Jews still waited for the Promised One—the King greater than King David.

And when the time was right, God prepared some very special people to welcome his Son.

Mary was a young Jewish woman.
Mary loved her village and the hills
around the little town of Nazareth
where she lived.

The morning dew felt cool on Mary's
toes as she walked to the well for
water.

"Good morning!" a voice interrupted
Mary's walk.

Mary looked around her.

"What? Who-o-o are you?" Mary
asked the stranger.

"I am the angel Gabriel, and God has sent me to tell you something important. The Lord has blessed you and is with you," said the angel visitor. Mary's mind was full of questions and confusion.

"Don't be afraid," the angel reassured her. "God is very pleased with you. He has chosen you to be the mother of the Son of God. Soon you will have a baby boy, and you will call him Jesus. He will be called great … and he will save the world."

"But how can this be?" said Mary, still confused. "I'm not married yet."

"God will cause a miracle to happen. With God all things are possible!"

Mary listened and believed the angel's words. "I trust the Lord." Mary knew this was a great blessing, and she began to sing praises to the Lord.

The angel also visited Joseph. He was a good man, and he loved Mary very much and was planning to marry her. The angel came to Joseph in a dream with the same message.

"God has caused a miracle to happen. Even though you aren't married, God's Holy Spirit has caused Mary to be pregnant. She will have a baby boy, and you will name him Jesus. Give him that special name, because it means he will save his people from their sins."

Joseph believed all that the angel said.

He was ready to obey. Mary was ready to obey. Together, they waited for the special miracle to come true.

While Mary and Joseph were waiting for this special miracle, they had to take a trip. They had to travel to a place called Bethlehem. The emperor said they had to go.

Joseph gently lifted Mary onto the donkey's back, and their journey began. "The Roman emperor picked a bad time to make us go to our hometowns!" Joseph complained.

"Yes," agreed Mary. "But it's the law. He wants to count his citizens."

The trip to Bethlehem was a hard journey for a woman about to have a baby. Late that night they reached the little town. "I'll find a room so you can rest," Joseph said.

But every inn he tried was full of people. He knocked on door after door, and got the same answer, "Full." "No more rooms." "Try down the street."

Joseph kept knocking and begging for a room. "Please, we'll take any little corner, anything you have. My wife is about to have a baby!"

The last innkeeper felt sorry for the young couple. "There's a stable in the back. It's small, dark, and with the animals. It's not very clean." "We'll take it!" said Joseph.

Joseph made Mary as comfortable as he could in the damp little stable— and not a moment too soon. For that night, her baby boy was born, just as the angel had said.

They named the baby Jesus. Mary looked at her beautiful baby, remembering the angel's words. "He will save the world."

That same night, some shepherds were taking care of their sheep in a nearby field. An angel of the Lord appeared to the shepherds, with a glorious light shining all around. The shepherds had never seen such a thing, and they were scared.

But the angel calmed them down by saying, "Don't be afraid. I am bringing you good news that will be a joy to all the people. Today your Savior was born in Bethlehem. This is how you will know him—he will be wrapped in cloths and lying in a manger."

Then many angels appeared in the sky, singing and praising God for the wonderful gift of baby Jesus.

They sang, "Glory to God in heaven, and on earth, peace and goodwill toward men!"

The shepherds could hardly wait to meet the baby Savior, so they went straight to town, looking for a baby lying in a manger. When they found Mary, Joseph, and Jesus, they knew that the angel's words were true.

That special baby, Jesus, grew up in a small town called Nazareth. For thirty years he lived an ordinary life with his family and friends. He had fun and he learned new things just like any other boy in Nazareth. Everyone knew him as the son of a carpenter.

Then one day, Jesus left his village and his ordinary life. He stepped into the world to do amazing and marvelous things in the name of God Almighty.

On the outside, Jesus really was like all the other young Jewish men in the village. But on the inside, he was very different. He was God's Son, and he had a special job to do.

When Jesus was a grown man and ready for his new job, he traveled to the Jordan River where his cousin John was teaching and baptizing people. John's strange appearance and important message were the talk of the countryside.

"Be baptized and turn your hearts to God!" John would preach. And many would listen and obey.

The banks of the river were covered with John's listeners.

Jesus joined them. Jesus made his way through the crowd. He walked to the shore of the river. He stepped into the deep blue waters of the Jordan and muddied his toes in the soggy riverbed.

Jesus knew that he was in the right place. His Father wanted him to begin his new job here, on the banks of the Jordan. And he needed his cousin John's help.

Jesus asked John to baptize him.

John protested, "No, you should baptize me!"

Jesus put his hand on John's shoulder and calmly replied, "It's OK. It is good for us to do this."

So there in the Jordan River, John baptized Jesus while all the other men and women watched from the shore.

While Jesus stood in the water, he began to pray. The heavens opened up. The spirit of God came floating down like a dove and rested on Jesus' shoulder.

Then a voice from heaven boomed through the countryside: "This is my Son whom I love. I am very pleased with him."

God spoke. He called Jesus his Son. Now the people knew what God had known all along—this carpenter from Nazareth was very, very special.

On that day, the ordinary ended and the spectacular began.

God wanted Jesus to go out and tell the people that he remembered his promise from long, long ago … that there would be a Messiah. And that he, Jesus, was that Messiah—that he was the Son of God.

And so it began … the once tiny baby all grown up, Jesus went out into the world.

To the people he became a prophet, a healer, a preacher, a friend—the Messiah they had waited for, for so long.